Colourful Austria

Colourful
Austria

Introduced by
Heinz Scheibenpflug

Historical notes by
Dr. Maria Neusser-Hromatka

Pinguin-Verlag, Innsbruck

For tabulating and checking the "Austrian down the centuries" section thanks are due to

Dozent Dr. O. Menghin
Univ.-Prof. Dr. Karl Pivec
Prof. Rat Dr. Maria Dawid

Front cover: the Hochschwab, Upper Styria
Back cover: Vienna, the Belvedere Park with S. Stephen's Cathedral in the background

Pen-and-ink drawings: Richard Ragonig;
English translations: Richard Rickett; French translation: Fred Geets

Lithographs: Fotolitho Longo, Frangart near Bozen; Druckerei Sochor, Zell am See; Tyrolia Innsbruck
and Ifolith, Innsbruck

Printed by Ueberreuter, Vienna
Printed in Austria
ISBN 3-7016-2319-8

At the heart of Europe

The pictures in this book are appropriately colourful and of an almost infinite variety, as befits a country that stretches from the mountains sloping down to Lake Constance in the west to Lake Neusiedl and the Hunagarian Plain in the east; from the granite uplands along the northern frontier to the precipitous limestone peaks of the far south. If present-day Austria is a household word, a decade or two ago it was no more than a question-mark, and before World War II it was still merely the puny remnant of an Empire, an Empire that though perpetuated by many monuments and insignia is to the present generation little more than a survival from the mists of antiquity, a theme of hallowed legends and a target of caustic criticism.

As Salvador de Madariaga once observed, Austria has more kilogrammes of history per square metre than any other country in the world. In this land, amid the colourful landscape of which this volume presents such a vivid impression, an almost infinite diversity of communities emerged and coalesced at a very early stage. The present volume also affords a brief but comprehensive survey of the dramatic developments and vicissitudes that have led up to the emergence of present-day Austria.

In the cultural domain this little country is of world-wide significance. It was on Austrian soil that the final act of the Nibelung saga was played out, that the Gudrun saga was woven, and that the cycle of Dietrich of Bern's sagas took shape. It was here too that Walther von der Vogelweide composed many of his loveliest "Minnelieder" songs, not to mention Oswald von Wolkenstein, the last exponent of this particular art.

Of Austria's array of writers, suffice it to mention names of the calibre of Franz Grillparzer, Peter Rosegger, Ferdinand Raimund and Adalbert Stifter, all of whom are secure of their place in the annals of the world's literature. Closely associated with them are the lofty standards of the Austrian theatre; and the Vienna Opera and Burgtheater, along with the Salzburg and Bregenz Festivals, are household words in the cultural world.

As for Austrian music, it circles the globe in the best sense of the term. Many of the great composers were either born in Austria or settled there: Mozart, Haydn, Beethoven, Schubert, Bruckner, Hugo Wolf and Mahler to name only a few. Austria was also the cradle of classical operetta as represented by masters such as Johann Strauss, Millöcker, Suppé, Lehár, etc. And was it not on the banks of the

Danube that the lilting Viennese Waltz was born, and Lanner's adaptations of popular old Austrian country-dances were perfected by Johann Strauss the Elder.

In the domain of Gothic art, Austria can boast scuptors of the stature of Anton Pilgram, the presiding architect of S. Stephen's Cathedral in Vienna, and of Michael Pacher, under whose hands wood seems to become a living organism. The opulence and beauty of Baroque can be claimed as virtually an Austrian monopoly, and it was the Baroque era that produced such great artists as Johann Bernhard Fischer von Erlach, Lucas von Hildebrandt and Jakob Prandtauer, sculptors like Raphael Donner, and painters like Daniel Gran, followed in the 19th and early 20th centuries by Waldmüller, Alt, Makart, Klimt, Schiele, Defregger and Egger-Lienz — again, to name only a few.

As well as being able to boast so many famous names in the artistic world, Austria is also noted for the quantity and quality of the inventors, research-workers and men of letters the country has produced, and Austrian universities and centres of learning enjoy a world-wide reputation.

For many centuries Austria has been a leading centre of European achievement and western civilisation, and this has had its effect on the Austrian people and their creative activities as well as on the country's urban and rural characteristics. Monasteries, castles, palaces, churches, historic sites, tillage, pastures and vineyards abound, as do industrial plants and gigantic power-stations that sometimes even invade the realms of eternal snow and ice. They have all left their mark on the Austrian landscape as well as on the Austrian people. From this diversity there has emerged a political unity that has managed to avoid uniformity. Even within the severely constricted frontiers of present-day Austria the characteristic features of the various Provinces have survived intact. Austria does not consist of Vienna alone, even if the capital is the home of some 25% of the country's population; and Innsbruck, not to mention Salzburg, can hardly be labelled "provincial" in the pejorative sense of the word. Even the tiniest and remotest villages have their own individuality since tourism brought them into contact with the out-side world.

Austria is not a big country, but it has a great deal to offer anyone who is prepared to explore it from end to end. Every little village has something worth spending time and trouble over. Age-old treasures are preserved and cherished. Folk-music, folk-dancing and folklore are kept alive for their own sakes and not just a tourist attractions. It is the same in the busy Festival centres as in the remotest skiing village half-buried under snow. Here and there, on the edge of the Burgenland puszta perhaps or at the extreme end of a long mountain valley, you can still enjoy a sense of utter remoteness, but in a matter of minutes you can be transported back to the social whirl if that is where your preference lies.

Attempts have been made to classify Austrians under three headings: wine, beer, and cider-drinkers. But three qualities all Austrians have in common: hospitality, sociability and good-humour. And there is little point in trying to classify Austrians as stock-types because their outstanding feature is individuality. They are also well aware that nothing is perfect or permanent in this world and therefore that nobody can keep beating his head against the wall, or always be right, or have any right to put other people right. On the contrary, it is esesntial to give yourself time to enjoy life, otherwise you will miss many of the good things it has to offer. Very many Austrians are blessed with an inborn musicality, a responsiveness to beauty and the arts that helps them to rise above material difficulties, which are only two of the reasons why Austria and its people are so much liked.

The three predominant colours in the Austrians palette are still the green of forest-clad Alpine slopes, the dazzling white of snow-clad peaks, and the azure blue of lakes. The foothills of the Alps are a mosaic of villages, manor houses and splendid monasteries nestling among meadows, pastures and leafy woods; while away from the mountains are an abundance of vineyards and gentle wine-clad slopes. And speaking of Austria's wealth of ancient cultural monuments, this is a hospitable land that welcomes visitors who come to appreciate its natural beauty and artistic treasures. Finally, present-day Austria's greatest virtue is the conviction that its bounteous heritage of natural beauty can be preserved for posterity, and that this small country at the heart of Europe still retains its individual personality.

Austria Down the Centuries

Late
Stone Age

Circa 40,000—circa 5000/4000 B. C.

Among a number of excavations of various kinds at Willendorf, in the Wachau, Lower Austria, were two female figures, one of which, the so-called "Venus of Willendorf" of oolitic limestone, has become world-famous: it is the most naturalistic of all the "Veneres" so far unearthed.

The Venus of Willendorf

Late
Stone Age
(neolithic)

Circa 5000/4000—1800 B. C.

Evidence of numerous peasant settlements in Burgenland, Lower and Upper Austria, in the Drau valley and in the Klagenfurt area.

Early
Bronze Age

Circa 1800—1300 B. C.

Historical and cultural development is determined by two main groups: the "Aunjetitz" civilisation abutting on to the northern part of Lower Austria, but not spreading southwards over the Danube except in its western area; and the "Straubing" civilisation in Vorarlberg, North Tyrol, Salzburg and Upper Austria.

The important feature of the "Straubing" civilisation was its exploitation of Alpine copper resources (ancient mine at Schwaz in Tyrol).

Late
Bronze Age

Circa 1300—750 B. C.

The urn-burial-grounds, found in Austria as well as in most other parts of Europe, have some historical connection (details of which are still unconfirmed) with the great Mass Migrations, and the migrations of the maritime peoples of the Eastern and Central Mediterranean.

Of particular significance are the early urn-fields of North Tyrol near Innsbruck (Wilten, Mühlau, Hötting, Sonnenburg-Natters, Völs, Volders) and the later excavations at Stillfried, Lower Austria, and Maria Rast (Lower Styria). The so-called "Kultwagen von Strettweg" discovered in a tumulus near Judenburg, Styria, belongs to the transition period leading to the Hallstatt civilisation proper.

The Hallstatt
Civilisation
(Early
Iron Age)

Circa 750—400 B. C.

Following the "urn-fields" came a group of civilisations named after the burial-ground near the town of Hallstatt in Upper Austria. From the interplay of various cultural streams, south-German and Venetian in particular, spreading in opposite directions there developed a definite "Hallstatt" civilisation almost identical in area with that of the later Province of Tyrol.

Bronze Kettle.
From Hallstatt

The wealth of Hallstatt was derived from salt-trading, and excavations reveal connections with various other groups. Further excavations at Dürrnberg near Hallein also confirm the important part played by salt-mining even in those early days. The Hallstatt tumuli of the "Wieser Gruppe" in Styria are obviously the burial-ground of a noble family.

The
La Tène
period

Circa 400—15 B. C.

During the 5th century B. C. the salt-mines at Dürrnberg must have been taken over by Celts of the early La Tène civilisation, who after peopling the Salzburg area thrust down the Danube at or shortly after the turn of the century. A century later they were spreading southwards through the Alps and founded the kingdom of Noricum with its centre in Carinthia. In Tyrol the

Youth from the Helenenberg

indigenous Hallstatt civilisation continued after assimilating elements of the La Tène civilisation. In 102 B. C. the Cimbri and Teutones passed through the land.

The Romans

15 B. C.—400 A. D.

In 15 B. C. the "Drusus campaign" led to the formation of the Roman province of Rhaetia, to which North Tyrol and Vorarlberg belonged. About the same time as the birth of Christ the kingdom of Noricum was peacefully penetrated and became a Roman province. Establishment of the first Danube frontier from Carnuntum to Boiodorum (Passau) as the northern limit of Roman expansion. Settling of the Province of Pannonia, extending from the eastern frontier of Noricum as far as the Hungarian north-south course of the Danube.

The Celtic town on the Helenenberg near Klagenfurt lasted till about the middle of the 1st century A. D. The highly impressive ruins of Carnuntum include two amphitheatres, a military camp, and a residential quarter (about 10,000 inhabitants probably).

166—180

War against the Marcomanni, who with the Quadi had overrun the Danube frontier. In 180 death of the Emperor and great military commander Marcus Aurelius (? in Vienna).

About 260 the Alemanni, who were constantly pouring over the Roman frontier on the Rhine, set foot for the first time on Austrian soil.

In 313 Christianity, which had been establishing itself in various localities ever since the start of the third century A. D., was declared by the Emperor Constantine to be the State religion. During the fourth century the dioceses of Aguntum near Lienz, Teurnia near Spittal on the Drau, and Virunum on the Zollfeld near Klagenfurt were established.

From about 400

The Austrian territories gradually withdrew from the Roman Empire.

434—453

The Huns under Attila occupy Pannonia and thrust further west, but on the death of Attila his Empire disintegrates.

500—600	By 500 the Bajuvars from the west were slowly beginning to infiltrate into the Danube area. After the withdrawal southwards of the Lombards in 568 came an invasion of the Avars from the east, followed by Slav tribes. Tyrol, which since the end of the Ostrogoth Empire in 553 had been loosely associated wit Italy, is now placed under the administration of a "Dux Raetiae".
	Towards the end of the sixth century the Bajuvars begin to take up defensive positions against the Slavs advancing up the Drau valley and along the Pustertal.
About 700	St. Rupert founds the Benedictine abbey of St. Peter on the ruins of Juvavum and is presented with the remains of the city by Archduke Theodore II of Bavaria.
696—805	The Bavarian bishopric at Salzburg and the Agilofing Archdukes of Bavaria set about Christianising the pagan Slav and Germanic tribes.
788	Bavaria and Carantania (Carinthia) are incorporated in the Empire of the Franks after the subjugation of Duke Tassilo III.
791—799	Charlemagne conquers the Avars and froms the "Ostmark" bounded by the rivers Enns, Raab, and Drau.
798—811	Salzburg, the intellectual centre of the Franco-Bavarian ecclesiastical province, is constituted an archbishopric under Bishop Arno.
881	Battle between the Franks and the Magyars at "Wenia". Annihilation of the Bavarian levies and disintegration of Charlemagne's "Ostmark" (907).
After 955	Defeat of the Magyars at Lechfeld and reconstitution of the "Ostmark" as a bulwark against them.
976	Elevation of Carinthia to the status of an independent Duchy under the House of Eppensteiner (1077).

1156	Austria is separated from Bavaria by Friedrich Barbarossa and created a hereditary duchy under the Babenberg Margrave Heinrich Jasomirgott.
1000—1093	Among the most important monasteries established by the Babenbergs are Melk (circa 1000), Göttweig (1074), Klosterneuburg (1114), Heiligenkreuz (1135), Admont (1074), Millstatt (1070), St. Paul im Lavanttal (1091), Wilten (1138), and Mehrerau (1093).
1077—1181	Construction of the castles Hohensalzburg, Hohenwerfen, and Petersberg near Friesach.

1130—
circa 1230

Erection of many Romanesque buildings in Salzburg and neighbouring territories. Reconstructions of Salzburg Cathedral after the fire of 1167. Re-building of the Abbey Church of St. Peter at Salzburg (1130—1140). Building of the Cathedral of Gurk in Carinthia with three naves and a crypt containing 100 pillars (1140—1200): of the Church and cloisters of Millstatt Monastery (1120—1170): of the basilicas of the Benedictine Abbeys at Seckau, Styria (1150—1164), and St. Paul im Lavanttal, Carinthia (1180—1230).

The crypt of Gurk Cathedral

Circa
1160—1200

The artistically-minded Babenbergs make their capital at Vienna, an important centre of Danube trade with the Orient, and situated on the route to the Holy Land taken by the first crusading armies. The Nibelung saga is woven into epic form, probably at Passau.

1220—1260

Late flowering of south-German Romanesque in the Danube lands: the west-front of St. Stephen's Cathedral in Vienna, with a wealth of figurative decoration above the doorway: the Great Door (1230—1260): the Romanesque naves of the Michaelerkirche in Vienna and of the Liebfrauenkirche at Wiener Neustadt (circa 1250).

1220—
circa 1300

First appearance of Gothic in Austria. For the Vienna Court of Leopold VI an architect from Burgundy designs the cloisters of Lilienfeld and Heiligenkreuz, the Babenberger ducal palace (almost entirely destroyed) at Klosterneuburg, and the "Capella speziosa", also at Klosterneuburg.

1246

Frederick the Quarrelsome, the last Babenberg, is killed fighting the Magyars under Bela IV on the battlefield of the Leitha.

1276—1282

Following his victory over King Ottocar of Bohemia on the Marchfeld in 1276, King Rudolf of Habsburg occupies the Babenbergs' lands and confers Austria and Styria on his son Albrecht, the beginning of the rule of the House of Habsburg.

1300—1340

The Albertine Choir of St. Stephen's Cathedral (1304—1340) and the Augustinerkirche (1340) in Vienna.

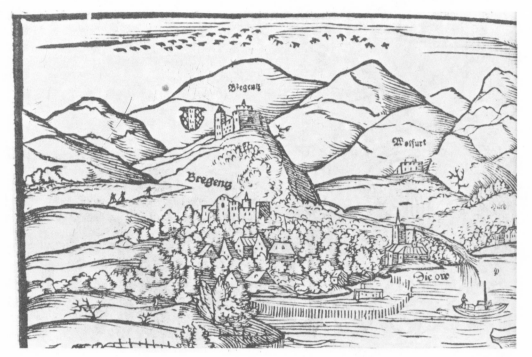

Bregenz

14

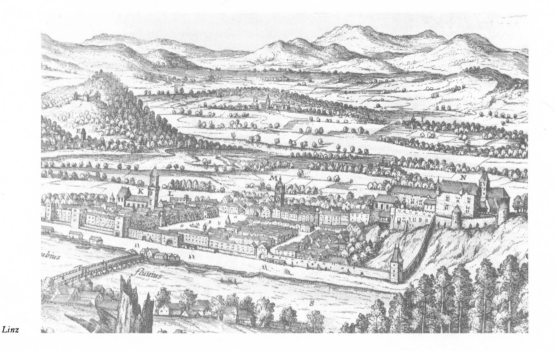

Linz

1300— circa 1340	The golden age of High Gothic sculpture and painting: the "Servants' Madonna" in St. Stephen's Cathedral, the Virgin at Klosterneuburg, the shrine of St. Florian in the Monastery of St. Florian, the Virgin and Child from the Monastery of Admont (in the Joanneum at Graz), and the Nonnberg crucifix at Salzburg.
1342	Margrave Ludwig of Brandenburg, husband of Margarethe Maultasch, issues the oldest known ordinance in Tyrol, the so-called "Grand Proclamation of Freedom", assuring equal political rights for all communities and individuals.
1349	The Great Plague.
1358—1365	Rudolf "the Founder" purports to have proof of Austrian sovereignty and claims the title of Archduke of Austria. Acquisition of Tyrol from Margarethe Maultasch (1365).
1359— circa 1440	The golden age of the Habsburg capital of Vienna unter Rudolf IV and the rulers in the Albertinian line.

15

1359—1467	Completion of the main aisle of St. Stephen's Cathedral, Vienna, which finally takes shape as a spacious edifice with three naves, three choirs, richly-ornamented pediments (1430) and a lofty, tapering south tower, the greatest example of German Late-Gothic in south-east Europe. The foundation-stone of the nave extension laid by Archduke Rudolf IV (1359).
1379	The partition of Austria between Rudolf's brothers Albrecht III and Leopold III, the former receiving Upper and Lower Austria, and the latter Tyrol, Styria, Carinthia, Krain, and the ancestral Habsburg domains on the Upper Rhine.
1380—1390	The Counts of Bregenz dispose of their rights in the Bregenzerwald and of their property at Feldkirch to the House of Habsburg (Leopold III).
1477	Acquisition of the Netherlands and the Franche-Comté of Burgundy through the marriage of the Archduke Maximilian, the son of the Emperor Friedrich III, to Maria, the only daughter of Charles the Bold.

Innsbruck

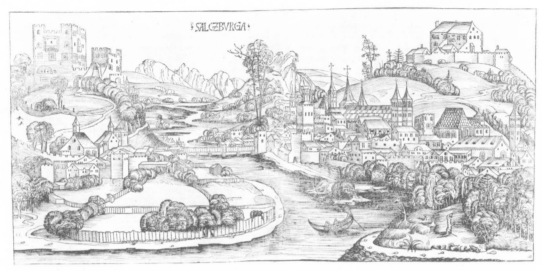

Salzburg

1480—1490	King Matthias Corvinus of Hungary occupies Lower Austria and Styria and attempts to rule his empire from Vienna during the years of famine 1480—1490.

The Emperor Friedrich III flees to Graz (the Burg dates from 1483), and from 1490 makes Wiener Neustadt, "the ever faithful," his capital, where the young King Maximilian is later received as liberator. |
| 1479—1519 | The great days of Tyrol, under Duke Sigmund "the rich in coin" and his relative and successor Maximilian (1490—1519). Innsbruck, the Emperor's favourite residence, is the seat of the "Upper Austrian" administration. Gun-foundry and Court armoury at Mühlau (from 1490). |
| 1481—1515 | The last days of Gothic and the dawn of a new era.

Triptych altar at St. Wolfgang by Michael Pacher. The Kefermarkt (Upper Austria) altar (1490—circa 1500). The marble tomb of the Emperor Friedrich III in St. Stephen's Cathedral, Vienna, as well as the base of the organ (1513) and pulpit (circa 1515) by the Cathedral architect Anton Pilgram. |
| 1497—1500 | Foundation of the Imperial "Hofkapelle" in Vienna by Maximilian I. |

1499—1515

The Habsburgs acquire an Empire by a series of shrewd marriages. Through Philip of Habsburg's marriage to Juana of Castile the Habsburgs acquire the Spanish Empire with its possessions in America and Naples (1499). Through the double marriage between Maximilian's grandchildren Ferdinand and Maria and the children of the Jagellon King, Ludwig and Anna, Bohemia and Hungary in due course pass to Austria.

Maximilian I

1500—1516

Acquisition from Bavaria of the mining districts of Kufstein and Kitzbühel; and of Lienz and the Gorizian territories on the Isonzo by the Emperor Maximilian. Organisation of the defence of Tyrol (conscription and local militia) by the "Landlibell" of 1511.

1508—1550

The Emperor Maximilian, as a "permanent memorial" to posterity, has his tomb, since become world-famous, prepared in the Hofkirche at Innsbruck.

Vienna

18

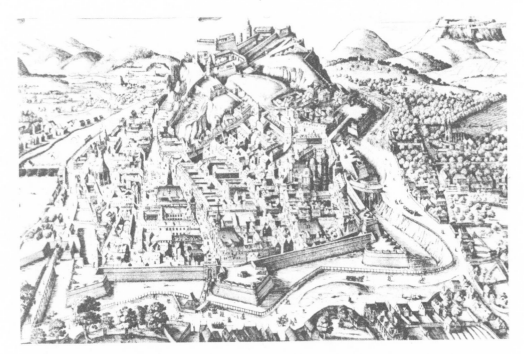

Graz

<table>
<tr><td>1522</td><td>The House of Habsburg separates into two distinct lines, Ferdinand receiving the Arch-Duchy of Austria above and below the river Enns, Styria, Carinthia, and Krain.</td></tr>
<tr><td>1526</td><td>The inherited territories of Bohemia, Silesia, and Hungary pass legally into the possession of Austria on the death of the last Jagellon King Ludwig II. Birth of the Danube Monarchy.</td></tr>
<tr><td>1529</td><td>Sultan Suleiman besieges Vienna, but is repulsed by Graf Niklas Salm-Reifferscheid.</td></tr>
<tr><td>1533</td><td>Vienna restored to its position as capital by Ferdinand I after a break of 100 years.</td></tr>
<tr><td>1541</td><td>Death in Salzburg of the famous doctor Theophrastus, the founder of medical chemistry.</td></tr>
</table>

19

1558—1566	Foundation of the Court Library and the Habsburg art collection.
1570—1580	The Emperor Maximilian allows the aristocracy in Upper and Lower Austria freedom of religion.
1571	The people of Vienna appeal for religious toleration.
1587—1612	Mediaeval Salzburg is transformed by Archbishop Wolf Dietrich into an Italianate Court residence. Widening of the Cathedral Square (1600) and enlargement of the archiepiscopal Residence (completed under Marcus Sitticus in 1619). Building of the Mirabell Palace and the memorial chaped to Wolf Dietrich in the cemetery of St. Sebastian.
1614—1628	Reconstruction of the Cathedral at Salzburg on the foundations of the former Romanesque basilica by Santino Solari in early Italian Baroque style. Solari also builds the country palace of Hellbrunn with its famous fountains (circa 1615).

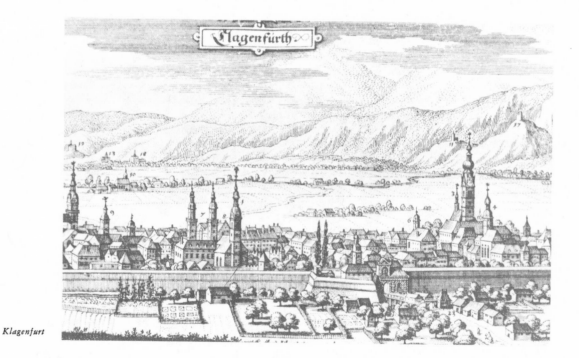

Klagenfurt

1640–1664	Lodovico Burnacini builds the first Imperial Opera House, seating 5,000 spectators.

1679 — According to contemporary, and probably exaggerated estimates, the Plague from Hungary claimed 100,000 victims in Vienna.

1683 — Vienna is again besieged by the Turks, this time commanded by the Grand Vizier Kara Mustapha. After a heroic defence by Graf Ernst Rüdiger von Starhemberg the city is relieved by an army coming down from the Kahlenberg, consisting of the Imperial forces and their Polish, Saxon, Bavarian, Swabian, and Frankish allies.

1697–1718 — After Prince Eugene's glorious victories over the Turks at Zenta (1697), Peterwardein (1716), and Belgrade (1717), Austria becomes the leading power in the Danube area. Further territories are acquired by the Treaty of Karlowitz in 1699 (Turkish possessions in Hungary, Transylvania, and parts of Croatia and Slavonia), and by the Treaty of Passarowitz in 1718 (the Banat, northern Serbia, and parts of Wallachia and Bosnia).

Prince Eugene

1695– circa 1740 — The heyday of Austrian Baroque, a product almost entirely of Austrian architects, such as Johann Bernhard Fischer von Erlach (1656–1723), Johann Lukas von Hildebrandt (1668–1745), Joseph Emanuel Fischer von Erlach (1693–1742), the Tyrolese Jakob Prandtauer (1660–1726), and the Court sculptor Meinrad Guggenbichler.

1714 — By the Peace of Rastatt the Bourbons are promised Spain. Spanish territories in Italy and the Netherlands (Belgium) are acquired by Austria.

1717 — Birth in the Vienna Hofburg of the Archduchess Maria Theresia, the last Habsburg ruler of genius, and founder of the Habsburg-Lothringen dynasty.

1732 — The final act of the Counter-Reformation: Archbishop Firmian of Salzburg orders the expulsion of 20,000 Protestants.

Maria Theresia

1732

On March 31, at the tiny village of Rohrau on the Leitha, Lower Austria, Joseph Haydn, the creator of the classical symphony and master of the classical string quartet, was born.

1740—1763

In the War of the Austrian Sucession (1740—1748) the Empress Maria Theresia resolutely defends her inheritance against the claims and attacks of Bavaria, Saxony, Prussia (Frederick the Great), and France. By the Treaty of Aachen she secures recognition of the Pragmatic Sanction, but is finally forced by the Treaty of Hubertusburg in 1763 to cede Silesia to Prussia.

1742—1780

Maria Theresia introduced many reforms, including the centralisation of the administration, the founding of the Military Academy, the reform of the army, compulsory education, and a new curriculum at the Vienna University, with lectures in German.

Joseph Haydn

1744—1780

Among examples of Maria-Theresia Rococo are: Schönbrunn Palace, the Empress' favourite residence, built by Nicolaus Pacassi (1744—1760), with its French-style park and its menagerie by Nicolas Jadot (circa 1750); and the Residence at Innsbruck, with its allegorical ceiling frescoes by Franz Anton Maulpertsch (1776).

1756

On January 27 Wolfgang Amadeus Mozart, son of the Court Kapellmeister Leopold Mozart, was born at Salzburg.

Circa 1760—1800

Wolfgang Amadeus Mozart

Vienna becomes a centre of music and the theatre, as well as of Grand Opera (Orfeo, by Christoph Willibald Gluck 1762), Italian opera buffa, and the German "Singspiel" (Mozart's "Die Entführung" in 1781 and "Die Zauberflöte" in 1791).

The Emperor Joseph II founds the "Deutsches Nationaltheater Burgtheater" on the Michaelerplatz, Vienna, in 1776 and the Josefstädter Theater, the first "popular" theatre, in 1788.

1780—1790	Among the reforms introduced by the Emperor Joseph II were: abolition of serfdom, the Edict of Tolerance, special status for the Jews, civil marriage, dissolution of monasteries, and the secularisation of Church property.
1795	Austria, Russia, and Prussia agree on the Third Partition of Poland, by which Austria annexes West Galicia and Cracow, and acquires the Bukovina by an agreement with Turkey in 1775.
1797	By the Treaty of Campo Formio (First Coalition war) between the Emperor Franz I and the French Directoire Austria loses Belgium and receives in compensation Venetia, Istria, and Dalmatia.
1806	Dissolution of the Holy Roman Empire. The Emperor Franz renounces its crown following the declaration of sovereignty by the Confederation of the Rhine under pressure from Napoleon. Adoption of the title of "Emperor of Austria" in 1804.
1809	Vienna occupied by French troops. Napoleon's first defeat at the bloody battle of Aspern (May 20, 1809). The new peace policy pursued by Fürst Clemens Metternich is consolidated by Napoleon's marriage to the Emperor's daugther Marie-Luise.
1809	Tyrol, anno 1809. Tyrol's heroic fight for freedom against the French and Bavarian occupying forces. A national uprising led by Andreas Hofer of Passeiertal clears the enemy out of Tyrol after three victories at Berg Isel. On Austria's being compelled to cede Tyrol by the Peace of Schönbrunn, Andreas Hofer resumes hostilities on his own initiative, but has finally to yield to superior forces and on February 20, 1810 is executed by the French at Mantua.
1814—1815	The Congress of Vienna establishes a new order in Europe dominated by the Conservative eastern powers, Russia, Austria, and Prussia. The territorial decisions of the Congress include Austria's renunciation of the Habsburg Netherlands (Belgium), and of the Habsburg properties on the Upper Rhine, but her retention of Tyrol, Vorarlberg, Lombardy, and Venetia, as well as her acquisition of the recently (1803) secularised Archbishopric of Salzburg.

Joseph II

Andreas Hofer

1815—1848

Franz Schubert

Fürst Clemens Metternich, the Austrian Chancellor and a leading European statesman of the day, presides over the destinies of the multi-racial Monarchy. At the centre of his "police State" is Vienna, an "intellectual Capua", the home of artists such as Ludwig van Beethoven (who lived and worked there from 1787 till his death in 1827), Franz Schubert, the first "Lieder" composer, and the waltz-kings Johann Strauss the Elder and Josef Lanner; the playwright and poet Franz Grillparzer, Ferdinand Raimund, with his popular pieces and fairy-stories, and Johann Nestroy, the popular actor and satirist. The leadings lyricist of this "Biedermeier" age was Nikolaus Lenau, with Adalbert Stifter as the principal epic poet.

1820—1850

Opening of the first Austrian railway, the Kaiser-Ferdinand-Nordbahn, in 1839.

1848
March 13.—15.

Revolution in Vienna, the Liberals demanding the end of the detested Metternich regime. Resignation and flight of Metternich.

April: Revolt in Hungary under Lajos Kossuth.

October 6: The October Revolution in Vienna is put down by Field-Marshal Windischgrätz. Triumph of the Conservatives, and military dictatorship of Fürst Schwarzenberg. Abdication of the Emperor Ferdinand, who is succeeded by Franz Joseph I.

1848/49

The Risorgimento in Italy. Field-Marshal Radetzky's victories in northern Italy, followed by reassertion of Austrian authority.

1859—1866

Unification of Italy. Sardinia and their French allies defeat the Austrians at Magenta and Solferino. Austria loses Lombardy and Venetia (1866).

Ludwig van Beethoven

1859—1869

Expansion of Vienna's city boundaries and razing of the bastions. Founding of the first great banks and of a free Press ("Neue Freie Presse"). Formation of the Sozialdemocratic party in 1868.

1866

End of the Austro-Prussian condominium. Following her defeat by Prussia at Sadowa Austria loses the hegemony of the German Confederation. Bismarck's astute policy of clemency refrains from imposing a territorial indemnity on Austria.

1873

World Exhibition in Vienna. The economic crisis leads to a slump on the Stock Exchange, and the failure of 125 new banks.

1856—1890

Vienna takes on the appearance of an Imperial capital: completion of the Ringstrasse.

The Age of Imperialism.

The Vienna of to-day takes shape, with the monumental buildings of Heinrich von Ferstel (the Votivkirche 1856—1879); the University; the Opera House by Siccardsburg and Van der Nüll, opened in 1869; the Court Museums, Hofburgtheater, and new wing of the Hofburg by Semper and Hasenauer; the new Rathaus and the church of Maria vom Siege by Friedrich Schmidt. Ceremonial statuary by Anton Fernkorn (the equestrian statues of the Archduke Karl and Prince Eugene); by Kaspar von Zumbusch (statues of the Empress Maria Theresia, Field-Marshal Radetzky, and Ludwig van Beethoven); and by Friedrich Helmer (Athene in front of the Parliament).

Johann Strauss the Younger

Circa 1860—1900

Music composed in Vienna includes the works of the last of the classical symphonists Johannes Brahms, who made Vienna his home from 1878 till his death in 1897; of the one-time organist at the monastery of St. Florian, Anton Bruckner; and of the master of classical operetta, Johann Strauss the Younger.

1900—1917

In the realm of science and technology, Julius von Wagner-Jauregg developed his epoch-making theory of the countering of progressive paralysis by malaria treatment (1917); and Sigmund Freud, the pioneer of psychoanalysis, published his theory of the origins of neuroses (1900).

1914—1918

June 1914; murder at Sarajevo of the heir to the Austrian throne, Archduke Franz Ferdinand, and his morganatic wife Duchess Sophie von Hohenburg.

July 28 1914; Austria declares war on Serbia and enters World War I at the side of her ally Germany.

October 1918; dissolution of the Dual Monarchy and creation of the "Successor States" (Czechoslovakia, Hungary, Yugoslavia, and Austria).

Eisenstadt 1618

1918	November 11; the last Emperor, Karl, renounces all his royal prerogatives. Proclamation in front of the Parliament building of the first Austrian Republic.
1919	By the Treaty of St. Germain the tiny Austrian Republic has to assume responsibility for the policy of the Habsburg Monarchy and cede all South Tyrol south of the Brenner Pass to Italy, as well as one or two areas in Lower Austria to Czechoslovakia.
1919—1920	Defensive operations against Yugoslav incursions, and a plebiscite in the areas of Carinthia occupied by Yugoslav forces, secure the province's retention by Austria. Inflation is mastered by the brilliant financial policy of Chancellor Ignaz Seipel.
1932—1934	Economic crisis in Austria. Frequent disturbances and occasional pitched battles between Marxist and National-Socialist armed formations. Dissolution of the National Assembly by Chancellor Dollfuss and banning of political parties. Foundation of the "Fatherland Front".
1934	July 25. Failure of a National-Socialist "putsch" in Vienna. Murder of Chancellor Dollfuss.

1938   March 13. Adolf Hitler occupies Austria and forcibly incorporates it in the "Third Reich". Vienna sinks to the status of provincial capital of the "Ostmark". The name "Austria" is "officially deleted from the map".

1939—1945   World War II draws to an end with the defeat of the German army at Stalingrad (1942/43) and the landing of British and American forces in Normandy (June 6 1944). Final defeat and capitulation of Germany.

1944   April 12. The first bombs fall in the area of "Greater Vienna".

1945   April 2. The Danube bridges blown up by SS troops. During the last days of the fighting in Vienna the Burgtheater and St. Stephen's Cathedral were destroyed by artillery fire. A month previously the Opera had been destroyed in an air-raid.

1945   April 13. Vienna falls to the Red Army after a five-day siege. The Austrian provinces are occupied by British, French, American, and Russian troops.

            April 27. Formation of a Provisional Government in Vienna under Chancellor Renner.

1945   April 27—May 10. The first post-war (Philharmonic) concert in the Grosser Musikvereinssaal in Vienna. The Vienna Burgtheater, playing in the Ronacher Theatre, re-opens with Grillparzer's "Sappho". The State Opera gives a performance of "Figaro" in the Volksoper. Opening of the University and high-schools.

1945   July 4. Restitution of the Austrian Republic based on the Constitution of 1920. Vienna divided into 4 sectors, and the provinces into 4 zones, of occupation.

1945/46   Vienna goes hungry: normal weekly ration 888 calories. The UNRRA famine relief scheme.

1948   Franz Lehàr, the famous composer of Viennese Operetta, dies in Bad Ischl.

1945/55   Reconstruction of St. Stephen's Cathedral by the Cathedral architect Holey. Reconstruction of the Opera to a design by Erich Boltenstern. Housing programme set on foot with international aid schemes.

	History	Culture

1955	May 15. Signature of the Austrian State Treaty in the Marmorsaal of the Belvedere Palace by the Foreign Ministers of Great Britain, France, Russia, and the USA, and by the Austrian Foreign Minister Leopold Figl.	
1955	October 25. The last soldier of the occupation forces leaves Austrian soil.	
1955		November 5. Re-opening of the Vienna Opera House with Beethoven's "Fidelio".
1957	September. The International Atomic Energy Agency makes Vienna its headquarters.	
1959	November 20. Austria joins EFTA.	
14 Dec. 1960	Austria a member of OECD.	
1960—1964		Renovation of the "Old" Festival Theatre at Salzburg.
8 Jan. 1964	Death of former Chancellor Julius Raab, the architect of the Austrian State Treaty.	
1964		Winter Olympic Games at Innsbruck.
1965	Dr. h. c. Franz Jonas elected President.	
Nov. 1966	Nikolai Podgorny, President of the Soviet Union, pays a State visit to Austria.	
1967	Vienna is the headquarters of UNIDO.	
Dec. 1971	Dr. Kurt Waldheim is elected Secretary-General of the United Nations.	
20—22 May 1972	On his way to a summit meeting in Moscow Richard Nixon, President of the United States, stops off in Austria, a further proof of the validity of Austrian neutrality.	
22 July 1972	The Austrian Chancellor Bruno Kreisky signs a Treaty of Association with the EEC at the Palais Egmont in Brussels.	
December 1973		Karl von Frisch und Konrad Lorenz receive the Nobel Prize.
July 1974	Dr. Rudolph Kirchschläger becomes President.	
1976		In February the Winter Olympic Games were held at Innsbruck for the second time.

History

15 May 1980	Ceremonies to mark the 25th anniversary of the signing of the State Treaty.
18 May 1980	Dr. Rudolf Kirchschläger again elected Federal President with a large majority.
1981	Austrian banks suffer multi-million losses in the greatest collapse of companies since 1945.
24 April 1983	Loss of the SPÖ overall majority at the general election. The FPÖ joins the Government as minor coalition partner.
8 June 1986	Dr. Kurt Waldheim elected Federal President.
21 January 1987	The Socialists (SPÖ) and the conservative People's Party (ÖVP) form a new Government.

Photographs and picture agencies

Photographs and picture agencies
Thanks are due to the following photographers and agencies for kindly making the pictures available (the numbers denote the pages on which they are featured):

Alpine Luftbild   73

Bildarchiv der Niederösterreichischen Landesregierung   55

Faustmann   71

Fremdenverkehrsstelle der Stadt Wien   34

Toni Federer   81

Albert Herndl   118

Hofstetter-Dia   50/51, 61, 65

Hans Huber   33, 35, 79

Otmar Kaiser   107

Landesbildstelle beim Amt der Steiermärkischen Landesregierung   120

Löbl   38/39, 41, 42/43, 45, 46/47, 52, 57, 58, 59, 70, 76, 78, 80, 88/89, 90, 92/93, 94, 95, 106, 108, 109, 110/111, 112, 113, 114, front cover, back cover

Magnum-Photos   44, 122/123

Mauritius Bildagentur   37, 53, 68, 82, 85

Heinz Müller-Brunke   40, 60, 62/63, 74/75, 86/87, 91, 116, 124/125, 127

Werner H. Müller   100

Landesfremdenverkehrsamt Burgenland   126

Österreichische Fremdenverkehrswerbung   54, 102, 121

Erik Pflanzer   56, 128

Hella Pflanzer   36, 48, 49, 64, 99

Pinguin-Bildarchiv   69

Fritz Prenzel   66, 67, 84

Albert Rastl   117

Risch-Lau   98

Toni Schneiders   77, 83, 97, 101, 103, 104/105, 119

Hans Senger   72

Thanks are due to the town of Dornbirn for permission to reproduce the lithograph on page 96

Der Stephansdom, das Wahrzeichen von Wien, vollendet 1433
St. Stephen's Cathedral, Vienna's most hallowed landmark, completed 1433
La cathédrale Saint-Etienne, symbole de Vienne, achevée en 1433

Das Benediktinerstift
Melk an der Donau.
Erbaut von Jakob
Prandtauer 1702–1726

The Benedictine Mon-
astery at Melk on the
Danube, built 1702–1726
by Jakob Prandtauer

Le monastère des
Bénédictins de Melk,
Danube. Construit par
Jakob Prandtauer,
1702–1726

oben
Altstadtgäßchen in Krems, Niederösterreich
Lane in the old part of Krems, Lower Austria
Ruelle dans la vieille ville à Krems, Basse-Autriche

rechts
Weingärten bei Zistersdorf, Niederösterreich
Vineyards near Zistersdorf, Lower Austria
Vignobles près de Zistersdorf, Basse-Autriche

Seite 80

Winter im Achental, bei Achenkirch, Tirol

Winter in the Achen Valley near Achenkirch, Tyrol

L'hiver dans l'Achental, Tyrol

Seite 81

Innsbruck, Morgensonne in der Altstadt

Early morning sunshine in the old quarter of Innsbruck

Innsbruck, la vieille ville sous le soleil matinal

oben

Erker an der reich bemalten Fassade des Gasthauses
Zum Stern in Ötz, Tirol

Oriel on the lavishly decorated façade of the Gasthaus
Zum Stern at Ötz, Tyrol

L'encorbellement de la façade richement ornée de fresques
de l'Auberge Stern à Ötz, Tyrol

rechts

Fiß, ein idyllisches Dorf im Oberinntal, Tirol

The idyllic village of Fiss in the Upper Inn Valley, Tyrol

Fiss, un idyllique village de la vallée de l'Inn supérieur,
Tyrol

links

Der Lindwurmbrunnen, errichtet 1590, das Wahrzeichen von Klagenfurt

The "Lindwurm" fountain (1590), the emblem of Klagenfurt

La Fontaine du Dragon, 1590, le symbole de Klagenfurt

rechts

Einer der schönen Bildstöcke, wie sie in Kärnten zahlreich zu finden sind

One of the many lovely wayside shrines in Carinthia

Voici une belle mont-joie, comme on en trouve beaucoup en Carinthie

Seite 110/111

Blick vom Koglereck ins Lavanttal, im Hintergrund die Saualpe, Kärnten

View of the Lavant Valley from the Koglereck: in the background the Saualpe

Vue de la vallée de Lavant prise du Koglereck, à l'arrière-plan la Saualpe, Carinthie

118

Seite 124/125
Ziehbrunnen und Schilfhütte in der „Pußta" des Burgen-
landes

Draw-well and reed-hut in the Burgenland "puszta"

Caractéristique paysage de la «puszta» du Burgenland, un
puits et une cabane de roseaux

oben

Segelboote auf dem Neusiedler See, Burgenland

Sailing boats on Lake Neusiedl, Burgenland

Voiliers sur le Lac de Neusiedl, Burgenland

rechts

Kleines Gaßl in Breitenbrunn, Burgenland

An alley at Breitenbrunn, Burgenland

Une ruelle à Breitenbrunn, Burgenland

In der Bergkirche in Eisenstadt fand Joseph Haydn seine letzte Ruhestätte,
Burgenland

Joseph Haydn's last resting-place in the Bergkirche at Eisenstadt,
Burgenland

C'est dans l'église d'Eisenstadt que se trouve la sépulture de Joseph Haydn,
Burgenland

Austria

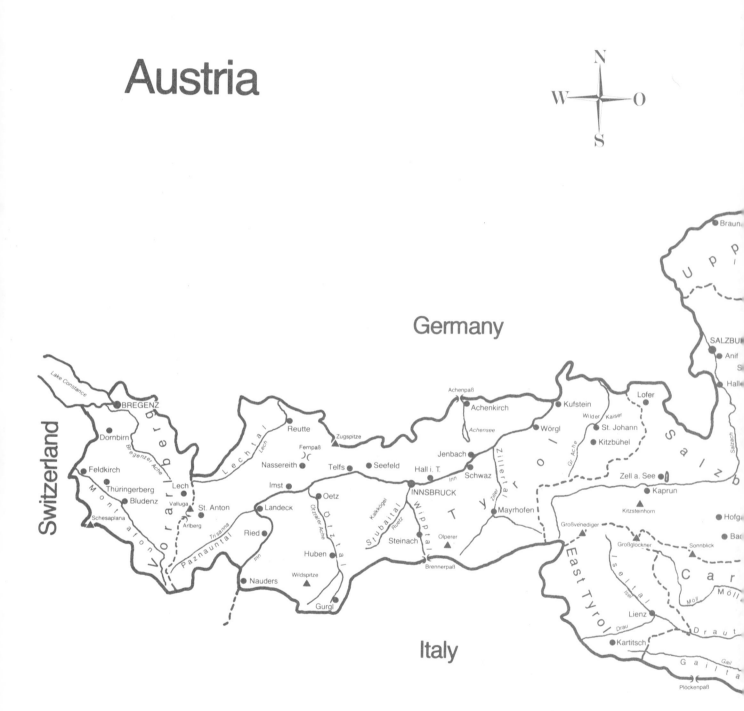

Germany

Switzerland

Italy